21st Century Skills Library

REAL WORLD MATH: SPORTS

SWIMMING

Cecilia Minden and Katie Marsico

Cherry Lake Publishing
Ann Arbor, Michigan

Published in the United States of America by Cherry Lake Publishing
Ann Arbor, Michigan
www.cherrylakepublishing.com

Math Adviser: Tonya Walker, MA, Boston University

Content Adviser: Thomas Sawyer, EdD, Professor of Recreation and Sport Management, Indiana State University

Photo Credits: Cover and page 1 and 4, ©iStockphoto.com/Purdue9394; page 6, ©iStockphoto.com/gertfrik; page 8, ©Andresr, used under license from Shutterstock, Inc.; page 10, ©iStockphoto.com/gertfrik; page 14, ©SportsWeb/Alamy; page 16, ©iStockphoto.com/kneafsey; page 18, ©AP Photo/Jay LaPrete; page 20, ©Chad McDermott, used under license from Shutterstock, Inc.; page 22, ©AP Photo/Mark J Terrill; page 25, ©PhotoCreate, used under license from Shutterstock, Inc.; page 27, ©Elena Elisseeva, used under license from Shutterstock, Inc.

TABLE OF CONTENTS

CHAPTER ONE

SPLASH!

Competitive swimmers need great timing, coordination, and an understanding of math to win races.

Yᵒᵘ stand strong on the edge of the pool. You have practiced every breath, stroke, and push for hours. This is your lane, your event, and it will be your win. The horn sounds, and you dive in. Your body glides through the water. You reach the end of the pool and turn. The crowd is cheering, but you have one goal. You must reach the other end of the pool before the other swimmers. The others are close. But with one last burst of energy, you touch the wall. You did it! You won!

Swimming has been around since the first person fell into a large body

of water. To survive, he began moving his arms and legs to get closer to the

shore. There are **ancient** pictures and carvings of people swimming more

than 5,000 years ago. Ever since that time, swimmers have used math to

measure how far and how fast they could swim.

REAL WORLD MATH CHALLENGE

Swim events are divided into two categories: a long course of 50 meters, and a short course of 25 meters. **What is the difference in distance between the two courses? How much longer is the long course than the short course? Give your answer in a percentage.**

(Turn to page 29 for the answers)

Competitive swimming is believed to have started in 1937 in

London, England. It became a part of the Olympic Games in 1896. Only

men were allowed to compete. The rules changed at the 1912 Olympics.

Since 1912, women have been competing in Olympic swimming events. These young women hold on to the starting blocks before a backstroke event.

Women were allowed to compete, and they have been winning races

ever since.

The Olympics continue to be a place where swimmers set official records.

Another major competition for swimmers is the FINA Swimming World Cup,

sponsored by the Fédération Internationale de Natation (FINA). The U.S.

team competes in both of these events. USA Swimming is their official sponsor.

Swim teams at the local level can be organized through community centers, neighborhood parks, and school groups. Local teams compete in leagues. USA Swimming rules apply to these leagues. There is no limit to the number of athletes on a team. Some leagues boast hundreds of members. You need math skills to count up all those swimmers!

Measuring meters and keeping track of time are only a few ways that swimmers use math. Grab your goggles and your towel. Let's dive into the wild world of swimming!

As interest in swimming increased, so did the need for bigger challenges. Swimmers found a creative way to test their skills by swimming the English Channel. This is a body of water between Great Britain and France. It stretches about 150 miles (241 kilometers) at its widest point.

The first person to swim the English Channel was Matthew Webb in 1875. It took him 21 hours and 45 minutes. Over the years, others have attempted it. The fastest person to swim the Channel was Petar Stoychev in 2007. It took him only 6 hours, 57 minutes, and 50 seconds. Alison Streeter is known as the Channel Champion. She swam the Channel 43 times! What do you think drives people to make this very challenging swim?

CHAPTER TWO

A Few Swimming Basics

Competitive swimming involves lots of exact measurements. Math is almost everywhere at a pool!

Many competition-sized pools are 50 meters (164 feet) long. The pool

is divided into equally spaced lanes using red, white, and blue lane

markers. The markers keep swimmers from swimming into each other.

The markers also keep waves and splashing to a minimum. There are lines

at each end of the lane markers. These tell the swimmer that the end of the lane is only 5 meters (16 feet) away. Some of the larger pools have

movable bulkheads, or partitions. These can be used to adjust the pool for

the 25-meter or 50-meter events.

REAL WORLD MATH CHALLENGE

Neva is swimming in the women's 1,500-meter freestyle race. A competition-sized pool is 50 meters (164 feet) long. **How many laps (lengths of the pool) does Neva need to swim to complete 1,500 meters?**

(Turn to page 29 for the answer)

Swim events are usually referred to as swim meets. Swimmers begin

by lining up at the starting block. This is an elevated box at one end of the

pool. The starting block slopes down so swimmers can dive smoothly into

the water. Swimmers must stand perfectly still on the starting block. If they

move even slightly, they can be disqualified. Swimmers refer to this as a

"DQ." When swimmers hear the starting horn, they dive into the water.

A lightweight cap that fits tightly over the head helps improve a swimmer's time.

A swimmer uses his whole body to push through the water. The water is pushing back. This is called **water resistance**. The less water resistance, the faster the swimmer can move through the water. This is why swimmers either shave off their hair or wear tight-fitting caps. Even swimsuit fabric helps to cut down on water resistance and increase speed.

Swim meets are divided into four categories based on **strokes**. Strokes are the swimming styles a swimmer uses. They include the butterfly, the breaststroke, the backstroke, and freestyle. There are separate events

for men and women. Within each category there are races of different

distances. The distance of a race can be 50 meters, 100 meters, 200 meters,

400 meters, 800 meters, or 1,500 meters. Here are general descriptions and

rules for each stroke:

The butterfly stroke was added to the Olympic Games in the 1950s.

It is the most difficult stroke to master. Think of a dolphin in the water.

Imagine the way it dips down and under. The swimmer's legs mimic this

movement while her arms pull her body forward.

The breaststroke is the oldest and slowest of the four strokes. The

swimmer's arms and legs stay under the water. They move at the same

time. This creates more water resistance. The swimmer uses powerful arm

muscles to push through the water.

In the backstroke, the swimmer alternates arm strokes while kicking with his feet. The swimmer may flip over to his stomach when turning, but he must end the race on his back.

A freestyle race means swimmers can choose whatever stroke they want. The most popular is the crawl. It is also the fastest. The swimmer's head stays in the water. She turns it to the side to breathe. The swimmer's arms are pulling her forward while her legs are kicking. This gives the swimmer a strong push toward the end of the pool.

A medley is a series of strokes. There is both an individual medley and a medley relay. In an individual medley, the swimmer begins with the butterfly. He then does the backstroke and follows with the breaststroke. He ends with freestyle. In a medley relay, each swimmer uses a different stroke. The first swimmer does the butterfly. The next one does the backstroke. The third does the breaststroke. The final swimmer gets to choose his stroke. The fastest swimmer on the team is usually the last one to swim.

Can you see how you need math skills to count and measure lanes, strokes, meters, and events? Another big way a swimmer uses math is to record time. Swimming is a sport of speed and **endurance**. The fastest swimmer is the winner. Time is calculated in minutes, seconds, and **centiseconds**.

Let's learn about some of the best swimmers and how they have used math to win the gold!

Johnny Weissmuller watched Australian swimmers using the crawl stroke. He created his own version for the 1924 Olympics. His innovation allowed him to become the first person to swim the 100-meter freestyle in less than 60 seconds! Thousands of swimmers have copied his style of swimming. Weissmuller is still considered one the most famous swimmers of all time. He swam in the Summer Olympics of 1924 and 1928. He won five gold medals! He later became an actor and played Tarzan in many movies.

CHAPTER THREE

DO THE MATH:
IMPRESSIVE PROS

One of the most impressive U.S. swimmers is Michael Phelps, a

swimmer from Maryland. At 15, he was the youngest swimmer ever to

qualify for the 2000 Olympics. It was no surprise when Phelps qualified

Michael Phelps of the United States is one of the world's best swimmers.
His technique combines strength, agility, and concentration.

again for the 2004 Olympics. He won four individual events, giving him four gold medals. He won two more gold medals as a member of relay teams, giving him a total of six Olympic gold medals. The only swimmer with more Olympic gold medals is another U.S. swimmer, Mark Spitz. Spitz holds the all-time record for having won seven gold medals in swimming at the 1972 Olympics. Spitz knows it is only a matter of time before someone beats that record. Maybe it will be Phelps.

At the 2007 World Championships, Phelps won seven gold medals. That was more than any other swimmer in World Championship history! With these amazing accomplishments, Phelps is arguably the greatest world-class swimmer today.

Phelps uses math to stay on a winning streak. He swims 6 to 7 days a week. He spends about 2 to 5 hours in the pool each day. Imagine

*Be sure to monitor your heartbeat when you exercise.
It's important to maintain a healthy heart rate.*

swimming 35 hours a week! Phelps does this to strengthen his heart.

Swimmers build endurance by keeping a steady heart rate during the race.

You can figure out your heart rate by placing two fingers on the inside

of your wrist. Can you feel the blood pumping? This is your heartbeat.

Now count how many beats there are per minute. Use the second hand on a watch to help you. A third-grade or fourth-grade student's heart rate should be 85 to 100 beats per minute. A swimmer's heart rate during competition can measure more than 200 beats per minute!

How do you read the numbers that show Phelps's record-breaking swim times? The minutes come first, the seconds are next, and the centiseconds come third. For example, at the 2007 USA Swimming Nationals, Phelps's time for the 200-meter backstroke was 1:54.65. That means he swam 200 meters in 1 minute, 54 seconds, and 65 centiseconds. World titles are sometimes determined by those tiny centiseconds!

REAL WORLD MATH CHALLENGE

Phelps is practicing for a big swim meet. He is entered in the 100-meter breaststroke. To build his endurance, he swims 10 sets of 100-meter stretches in 2 minutes. **How many total meters is Phelps swimming? How many meters is Phelps swimming each minute?**

(Turn to page 29 for the answers)

*American distance swimmer Kate Ziegler takes part in
the 200-meter freestyle event at a 2008 meet.*

Another U.S. swimmer who combines math and talent is Kate Ziegler.

She trains by swimming 1,100 meters a day, 6 days a week. All that training

pays off.

Ziegler has been breaking records since she hit competitive waters.

She began by breaking Cynthia "Sippy" Woodhead's 800-meter freestyle

record at the 2004 FINA World Cup in New York. In 2005, she was ranked

first in the world in both 800-meter and 1,500-meter freestyle. She beat her own 800-meter time with an 8:18.52 in March 2007. Ziegler's best time for the 100-meter freestyle was recorded at 56:60 in 2007. That means she swam the length of a 50-meter pool and back in less than a minute!

As you can see, smaller numbers add up to big wins!

21st Century Content

Swimming has been a part of the Olympics since 1896. The first competitions were underwater swimming, obstacle swimming, and plunge for the distance. They were held in open waters. Swimming today takes place in carefully measured pools. It uses strict guidelines. One thing hasn't changed. Athletes gather from all over the world. The Olympics provides a place where all nations can come together in peace.

REAL WORLD MATH CHALLENGE

U.S. team member Janet Evans set a world record of 15:52.10 in the 1,500-meter freestyle in 1988. Ziegler beat that record in 2007 with a time of 15:42.54. **How many years did Evans hold the world record for the 1,500-meter freestyle? How much better was Ziegler's time than Evans's time?**

(Turn to page 29 for the answers)

Do the Math: Remarkable Swimming Records

The difference between winning and losing a swim race can be a matter of centiseconds.

Sixty percent of all current swimming records were set between 2005 and 2007. Many of these records will change by the time you read this book. Things change quickly when the difference between first and second place is measured in centiseconds!

A swimmer's biggest **opponent** is the clock. Knowing he might beat a world record often gives a swimmer that extra push. He knows he needs to get through the water as fast as possible to beat the times of other swimmers. While there are many swimmers on each team, only eight swimmers get to compete in a race. To qualify, a swimmer must have the best time for a certain event.

U.S. swimmers hold many world records. Phelps holds four world records. Brendan Hansen broke previous records in 2006 with a 59.13 in the 100-meter breaststroke. Eight months later, he earned his second world record with a 2:08.50 in the 200-meter breaststroke.

Natalie Coughlin won four gold medals at the 2004 Olympics. Coughlin is talented in many different events. She qualified in the 100-meter butterfly, the 100-meter backstroke, and the 100-meter freestyle.

*Olympic gold medalist Natalie Coughlin competes
in the 100-meter backstroke event.*

She also holds a world record for the 100-meter backstroke. Kathryn Hoff

holds the world record for the 400-meter individual medley. Remember,

that means she used four different strokes to swim 400 meters. She did it

in 4:32.89!

International swimmers have broken records, too. Australia is one of

the United States' biggest rivals in competitive swimming. Australian Libby

Lenton placed first in both the 50-meter and 100-meter freestyle at the

2007 FINA World Championships.

Australian women also hold the world record for the 4 x 100-meter

medley, too. Think about that. It involves four women, each swimming a

different stroke, and each swimming a distance of 100 meters. And they

completed the medley in less than 4 minutes. Math skills will help you

figure out that each woman swam less than 1 minute!

REAL WORLD MATH CHALLENGE

At the 2004 Summer Olympics, the Australian women's team swam the 4 x 100-meter medley in 3:35.94. **How many minutes is this? How many seconds? How many centiseconds? What was the average number of seconds it took each woman to swim her lap?**

(Turn to page 29 for the answers)

Swimmers stay motivated to do their best when they understand their own learning needs. This is especially true for athletes in the Paralympics. The Paralympics are for athletes with physical disabilities. Athletes with physical disabilities often must adapt their techniques to overcome those disabilities. Clodoaldo Silva from Brazil is just one of the many athletes who have overcome disabilities to excel at their sport. Cerebral palsy didn't stop him from winning six gold medals and one silver medal at the Athens 2004 games. He also set four world and five Paralympic records.

When you think about it, every swimmer in a competition is pretty remarkable. Use your math skills to imagine the hours these athletes spend in the pool swimming laps. Many of those hours pay off in record-setting wins. All of those hours pay off in becoming a skilled athlete.

REAL WORLD MATH CHALLENGE

At the 2004 Olympics, the U.S. men's 4 x 100-meter relay team set a world record time of 3:30.68. Germany set a European record of 3:33.62. Japan set an Asian record of 3:35.22. **What is the time difference between the U.S. and German teams? What is the time difference between the German and Japanese teams? What is the time difference between the U.S. and Japanese teams?**

(Turn to page 29 for the answers)

CHAPTER FIVE

GET IN AND SWIM!

Joining a local swimming league or club is one way to dive into the world of competitive swimming.

Y ou can become a competitive swimmer by joining a swim league. Start with your city or school leagues.

You may also find swim leagues at the local YMCA. You don't need a lot of equipment. A swimsuit, goggles to protect your eyes, and a cap to cover your hair will get you started.

The biggest expense for swimming is time. We've read how many hours each week the top swimmers are in the pool. They also lift weights, run, and bike to build endurance. Are you ready to put in the extra hours for your workout? Most coaches will tell you that preparation is half the battle. All those hours working out give swimmers the strength they need to make that last push to the wall.

You can begin by swimming laps at your favorite pool. An outdoor pool is great for sunshine, but an indoor pool allows you to swim year-round. Avoid injury by doing some simple warm-up stretches before jumping in. Some swimmers do stretching exercises outside the pool. Others swim slowly for a few laps. Choose which warm-up plan is right for you and get moving.

You may want to experiment with all four strokes until you find the one that works best for you. Once you've found "your stroke," practice it often. Each time you swim, push yourself a bit harder to do one more lap.

Swimming can also be about having fun with your friends in the water.

Maybe a friend is willing to swim in the lane next to you. A little friendly

competition never hurt anyone!

Ask someone to time your laps. Keep a chart of your times. You will

probably discover that the more you work out, the less time it takes to

swim each lap.

Swimming isn't always about competition. Hanging out at a pool

with your friends is a great way to cool off on a hot summer day. Other

people like open-water swimming. They head to the beach and let the

Swimmers use a lot of energy during workouts and competitions. It is important for them to make healthy decisions about their diet. The Food Pyramid is a good model for healthy eating. Grains, vegetables, and fruits are the best foods to fuel swimmers. Whole grain breads and pastas, oatmeal, beans, and bananas are all great sources of the complex carbohydrates that swimmers need for energy.

For more information on the Food Pyramid and healthy eating, visit www.mypyramid.gov.

ocean waves roll them back to shore. Water parks are becoming more popular every year. Huge slides and wave pools give you a chance to get wet and have fun.

Whether you choose to swim in the ocean or go for the gold, you can use math to measure distances and keep track of your time. So what are you waiting for? Jump in and start swimming!

REAL WORLD MATH CHALLENGE

The Price family wants to buy tickets for swimming events at the Olympics. Mr. and Mrs. Price want 2 tickets for the men's 400-meter freestyle final. Tickets are $300 each. Their daughter wants to see the women's 100-meter butterfly final. Mrs. Price will go with her. Tickets are $325 each. All three of the Price family members want to see the men's 4 x 200-meter freestyle relay. Tickets are $400 each. **What is the total amount that the Price family will spend on tickets for Olympic swimming events?**

(Turn to page 29 for the answer)

REAL WORLD MATH CHALLENGE ANSWERS

Chapter One

Page 5

The difference between the two courses is 25 meters.

50 meters − 25 meters = 25 meters

The long course is 50 percent longer than the short course.

25 ÷ 50 = 0.50 = 50%

Chapter Two

Page 9

Neva needs to swim 30 laps.

1,500 meters ÷ 50 meters = 30 laps

Chapter Three

Page 17

Phelps swims a total of 1,000 meters.

10 sets x 100 meters = 1,000 meters

He is swimming 500 meters every minute.

1,000 meters ÷ 2 minutes = 500 meters per minute

Page 19

Evans held the world record for the 1,500-meter freestyle for 19 years.

2007 − 1988 = 19 years

Ziegler beat the record by 9.56 seconds.

15:52.10 − 15.42.54 = 9.56 seconds

Chapter Four

Page 23

The Australian women's team swam the 4 x 100-meter medley in 3 minutes, 35 seconds, and 94 centiseconds.

The number of seconds each woman swam was 53.75.

3 minutes x 60 seconds = 180 seconds

180 seconds + 35 seconds = 215 seconds

215 seconds ÷ 4 swimmers = 53.75 seconds

Page 24

The time difference between the U.S. and German teams is 2.94 seconds.

3:33.62 − 3:30.68 = 00:02.94

The time difference between the German and Japanese teams is 1.60 seconds.

3:35.22 − 3:33.62 = 00:01.60

The time difference between the U.S. and Japanese teams is 4.54 seconds.

3:35.22 − 3:30.68 = 00:04.54

Chapter Five

Page 28

The Price family will spend $2,450 on Olympic tickets.

$300 x 2 = $600 for the men's 400-meter freestyle final

$325 x 2 = $650 for the women's 100-meter butterfly final

$400 x 3= $1,200 for the men's 4 x 200-meter freestyle relay

$600 + $650 + $1,200 = $2,450 total

Glossary

ancient (AYN-shunt) dating back thousands of years

centiseconds (SEN-tuh-seh-kundz) units of measurement that make up one hundredth of a second

competitive (kuhm-PEH-tuh-tiv) the efforts of two or more parties to win a sporting event

endurance (in-DUR-ents) the ability to keep up intense exercise or activity over an extended period of time

opponent (uh-POH-nuhnt) someone who is against you in a contest or athletic event

strokes (STROHKS) a series of arm movements against the resistance of the water

water resistance (WAH-tur ri-ZISS-tuhnss) an opposing force of water

For More Information

Books

Fischer, David. *The Encyclopedia of the Summer Olympics*. New York: Scholastic, 2004.

Mason, Paul. *How to Improve at Swimming*. New York: Crabtree Publishing Company, 2008.

Web Sites

Official Site of USA Swimming
www.usaswimming.org
For the latest updates and news about the U.S. swim team and its swimmers

Swim Info: Swimming World Magazine
www.swimmingworldmagazine.com
Get the inside scoop on the world of competitive swimming

INDEX

ABOUT THE AUTHORS

Cecilia Minden, PhD, is a former classroom teacher and university professor. She now enjoys being a literacy consultant and author of children's books. She lives with her family near Chapel Hill, North Carolina. She would like to thank Ron Price for sharing the insight he gained during his 20 years as a swimming and diving coach in Charlottesville, Virginia.

Katie Marsico worked as a managing editor in children's publishing before becoming a freelance writer. She lives near Chicago, Illinois, with her husband and two children. She loves to swim, preferably in the Gulf of Mexico or the Caribbean.